Integrating Virtual Reality in HR

Enhancing Recruitment and Selection

Table of Contents

Chapter 1. Introduction

Welcome to this exclusive Special Report entitled "Integrating Virtual Reality in HR: Enhancing Recruitment and Selection". Within these pages, you will discover the transformative potential of Virtual Reality (VR) in the realm of Human Resources. We take you on a journey from the nascent stages of VR technology in HR to its current and future applications, particularly in the field of recruitment and selection. Our report is rich with real-world examples, expert opinions, and strategic guidelines, all carefully pieced together to give you the best picture of this exciting intersection of technology and talent management. There's never been a better time to explore this burgeoning trend that's set to revolutionize how we attract, assess, and select talent in the modern business landscape. By the end of this report, you'll be more than just conversant—you'll be ready to reshape your HR strategy for a more engaging, efficient, and immersive future. Onboard this thrilling exploration of VR in HR, and let's together trailblaze the path of innovative recruitment and selection!

Chapter 2. The Dawn of Virtual Reality in HR

Virtual reality might not immediately spring to mind when you think about HR—after all, it's a technology more readily associated with gaming and video entertainment. Nevertheless, the VR tide has started to turn, and HR departments across the globe are now harnessing the technology to revamp and reimagine their processes.

2.1. Locating Virtual Reality in HR

The journey of VR into HR did not happen overnight. The introduction was gradual and cautious, with many pioneers often referring to it as an experimental tool in its early stages. However, as the technology matured, so did its application in HR. Today, VR is not only used for training and development but is also finding a central place in HR's recruitment and selection sphere.

VR is a technology that allows people to immerse themselves in a computer-simulated, three-dimensional environment. This immersive aspect makes VR a highly practical and interactive tool, allowing potential employees to experience the realities of a job, without having to leave their homes.

2.2. The Catalysts of VR Adoption in HR

Several factors have contributed to the increasing adoption of VR technology in HR. Among the key catalyzers for VR's entry into HR are the advancements in technology that have made VR more affordable and more accessible. Besides the drop in hardware prices, the emergence of cloud-based VR solutions has played a pivotal role, enabling organizations to implement this innovative tech without requiring heavy upfront capital investment.

Furthermore, the advent of 5G mobile technology promises to push VR usage in HR even further. With faster speeds and lower latency, 5G will provide a lag-free virtual environment, making the VR experience more seamless and enjoyable.

Another crucial catalyst has been the sudden shift towards remote work, spurred by the global pandemic in 2020. With traditional face-to-face interviews and recruitment sessions now a distant memory for most companies, the need for virtual alternatives has soared—making virtual reality a timely solution.

2.3. Early Adoption of Virtual Reality in HR

In the early stages, VR usage was primarily limited to training and development. Big corporations in industries such as aviation, medicine, and the military, were some of the earliest adopters. Flight simulators in aviation and combat scenarios in military training are iconic examples of how VR has long been utilized to provide safe and controlled training environments.

Soon, as the technology became more affordable, companies across sectors started incorporating VR in their training programs. For instance, Walmart has been using VR to train their employees on complex processes and customer service since 2017. This immersive training enables employees to learn and adapt in a life-like but risk-free virtual environment.

2.4. VR Breaches the Field of Recruitment and Selection

The leap from training to recruitment and selection was a logical and intuitive one. If VR could effectively simulate the work environment for training, it could just as easily help prospective employees understand the organization's culture, work environment, and job requirements during the recruitment process.

Several companies started integrating VR into their recruitment strategies to showcase their workspaces and company cultures. For example, General Mills started offering virtual plant tours to candidates so they could experience the working environment before their in-person visit.

Likewise, L'Oreal developed a VR experience to allow candidates to step inside their offices virtually. Such initiatives not only helped candidates become more familiar with the workplaces they would potentially be joining, but also served as a testament to the companies' innovation and tech-savviness, boosting their employer branding in the process.

While in the realm of selection, VR has started to play a significant role in skill assessment. Companies like Jaguar Land Rover and DHL have used VR to assess a candidate's skills and aptitude for specific roles. VR-based assessments can provide an immersive, interactive, and realistic way for candidates to demonstrate their capabilities, thus providing recruiters with more reliable and holistic evaluation metrics.

In the academic sector, Michigan State University researchers created a VR-based interview training tool to help job candidates hone their interview skills. This VR tool provides candidates with immediate feedback, helping them iron out the wrinkles before their actual interview.

2.5. Looking Ahead: The Future of VR in HR

The future of VR in HR looks exceptionally promising. Trends indicate a continuous growth of VR in HR with more potential for innovations. As VR technology becomes more prevalent and mainstream, it will inevitably become a default component of the HR technology toolkit.

Especially in the recruitment and selection arena, VR has the potential to transform the way companies attract, assess, and engage potential employees. With the evolving workplace, where remote work and digital connectivity are the norms rather than the exception, the entry of VR could not be timelier.

The dawn of VR in HR is a game-changing moment that's not merely illuminating novel approaches to training, recruitment, and selection, but also sparking a broader transformation within HR itself. As we delve deeper into how VR is reshaping the global HR landscape, we stake our claim at the cusp of what promises to be an HR revolution powered by virtual reality.

Chapter 3. Understanding the Basics: Virtual Reality Terminology

Before we delve into how virtual reality is changing HR and recruitment, it's crucial to understand the terminology associated with this technology. Our journey begins here.

3.1. What is Virtual Reality (VR)?

First, let's define Virtual Reality or VR. VR is immersive technology that creates a simulation of an alternate three-dimensional environment users can explore and interact with. Using specialized hardware such as headsets and gloves, VR provides an immersive experience that tricks the human brain into believing it is existing in a virtual world.

3.2. Components of VR

VR technology comprises several foundational elements. These range from the hardware and software that power the VR platform to the perceptual factors that help achieve full immersion.

- Hardware: VR hardware typically includes a headset, which might consist of a head-tracked display and headphones for sound, and peripherals like gloves or handheld controllers. These tools capture the user's movements and send them to the computer.

- Software: This includes the VR application running the simulation. Here, developers may create environments from scratch or recreate existing locations from the real world.

- Immersion: VR thrives on creating the illusion of immersion. This involves developing an environment that convinces our senses that we're interacting with a physical world.

- Interaction: Interaction is central to the VR experience. It could range from simple movements like looking around or walking to complex tasks like manipulating virtual objects.

3.3. Types of VR

The VR landscape is quite complex, featuring different types with varying capabilities.

- Fully Immersive: As the name suggests, fully immersive VR provides a highly realistic experience using high-resolution graphics, a wide field of view, high refresh rates, and effective sound and tactile feedback.

- Semi-Immersive: Semi-immersive VR still offers an immersive experience, but not to the extent of full immersion. This approach benefits from the use of physical environments to supplement the virtual.

- Non-Immersive: In non-immersive VR, the user remains aware of their real-world surroundings. This often includes simulations run on a desktop.

3.4. Senses Involved in VR

Virtual reality employs our key senses to create an immersive experience. Let's explore how these senses come into play:

- Vision: The predominant sense used in VR, vision, is catered through 3D graphics creating a life-sized, three-dimensional virtual environment.

- Sound: 3D sound or spatial audio is used to mimic the way

humans receive sounds from different directions, aiding in immersion.

- Touch: Haptic feedback technology delivers tactile responses to users, mimicking the feel of real objects or environments.

- Smell and Taste: Though not as common, some systems also aim to trigger these senses for a truly holistic VR experience.

3.5. Common VR Terminology

Understanding different terms associated with VR can help you better grasp how the technology works. Here are a few common terms:

- Head-Mounted Display (HMD): A device worn on the head that presents images and sound for the immersive experience.

- Tethered: This refers to VR headsets that require a physical connection (or tether) to a computer or game console.

- Standalone: These are VR headsets that operate without the need for an external device.

- 360-Degree View: A VR feature that enables the user to look in any direction in the virtual environment, as they would in real life.

- Field of View (FoV): The extent of the observable environment at any given moment.

- Latency: The delay between the user's actions and the response or reaction within the VR environment. Low latency is essential for a convincing VR experience.

- Haptic Feedback: Technology that uses touch through vibrations or motions to provide feedback to users.

- 6DoF (Six Degrees of Freedom): Refers to the ability to move freely in any direction: up, down, left, right, backward, and forward.

By now, you should be well-versed in the terminology associated with Virtual Reality. As we move forward in this report, we will explore how these terms and the principles they represent apply more directly to HR's recruitment and selection processes. We hope this has set a solid foundation for truly appreciating the potential VR holds for revolutionizing talent management.

Chapter 4. Exploring the Role of VR in Talent Acquisition

Virtual Reality (VR) is a cutting-edge technology that has the potential to completely revolutionize the way companies recruit and select candidates. This transformative tech immerses users into digital worlds, enabling businesses to approach talent acquisition in innovative, immersive, and highly impactful ways.

4.1. The Emergence of VR in Talent Acquisition

The use of VR in talent acquisition didn't materialize overnight. The integration of this technology has been gradual, evolving alongside broader advancements in digital, remote, and immersive technologies. It all began with simple 360-degree tours of office spaces but quickly expanded into much more dynamic and interactive experiences.

In 2014, Facebook purchased Oculus VR, signaling the tech giant's confidence in the future of VR technology. In the same year, the British Army employed VR for recruiting purposes, providing a virtual experience of various roles within the military. The following years saw a sharp rise in the application of VR in HR, with many pioneering organizations recognizing its potential for talent acquisition. Today, VR is utilized by companies across various industries, including education, healthcare, and manufacturing, all aiming to bring a new dimension to the recruitment and talent acquisition process.

4.2. Benefits of VR in Talent Acquisition

VR brings a host of benefits to the realm of talent acquisition. For starters, it allows companies to provide much richer and immersive experiences than traditional job descriptions or interviews. This immersive engagement is particularly useful when trying to attract top-notch talent in a competitive job market.

Through virtual reality, companies can paint a vivid picture of what it's like to work for them, showcasing their work environment, culture, and values in a way that words or even videos simply can't capture. Candidates can virtually explore the office, meet potential colleagues, and even experience a day in the life of their prospective job. This immersion forms a profound emotional connection, promoting a strong employer brand and candidate attraction.

Moreover, VR functionalities can serve as innovative assessment tools. Custom scenarios and simulations allow recruiters to assess a candidate's skills, competencies, and suitability for a role much more holistically than through typical one-dimensional assessments. Candidates can demonstrate problem-solving skills, team collaboration, or how they handle stressful situations in real-time, while organizations gain valuable insights far beyond what a resume can provide.

Lastly, the use of virtual reality can make the recruitment process more efficient and cost-effective. By enabling remote, virtual visits, and immersive assessments, companies can streamline recruitment, without the limitations of geographical boundaries.

4.3. Implementation Challenges and Solutions

Of course, the integration of VR into talent acquisition is not without challenges. There are cost considerations, technical complexities, and the need for specialized skills to create and manage VR content.

However, solutions are emerging. Cloud-based VR services can reduce initial outlays, making the tech more affordable for businesses. Off-the-shelf VR applications, offering ready-made environments suitable for various industries, are also becoming more prevalent. Furthermore, as more and more businesses invest in this technology, there is an increasing pool of freelance VR developers and service providers available to support companies' VR endeavours.

4.4. Case Study: Deutsche Bahn

In a need to recruit thousands of workers to replace those heading towards retirement, Deutsche Bahn turned to VR. The German rail company offered potential applicants a chance to virtually experience a wide variety of jobs within their company. From a virtual tour of a signalman's tower to a simulation of an electrician conducting a maintenance check on a train, candidates could not only learn about the roles available but could 'try out' these roles in a virtual environment.

The result was an influx of applicants. With the VR initiative, Deutsche Bahn successfully managed to attract a significant number of potential employees to explore and engage with their brand. The initiative's success underscored the potency of VR as a tool for talent acquisition.

4.5. Future Context: Enhancing VR with AI and Big data

The future of VR in talent acquisition looks bright as it intertwines with other innovative technologies. Artificial Intelligence (AI) and big data, for instance, can elevate the potential of VR in ways unimaginable.

AI can imbue VR environments with autonomous, interactive characters that react realistically to the actions of the user. Intelligent systems can even adapt VR scenarios based on the ongoing performance and responses of participants, providing a truly personalized recruitment experience.

Meanwhile, big data analytics can offer deep insights from the wealth of data generated during VR activities. Companies could analyze how candidates react in real-time to certain situations, how they approach and solve problems, and how they make decisions. These valuable insights could significantly enhance the accuracy and precision of talent selection, fostering more informed and effective recruitment decisions.

4.6. Conclusion

In conclusion, VR holds immense potential to disrupt and enhance talent acquisition. While the initial investment and ongoing management may warrant serious consideration, the potential gains—enhanced candidate experience, better talent assessment, increased efficiency, and cost savings—make a compelling case for integrating VR in HR strategy.

The success stories emerging from forward-thinking companies solidifying VR's place in HR combined with the advent of affordable and accessible VR platforms underscore that VR is not merely a fancy future projection—it is a tangible, impactful tool of today's talent acquisition landscape.

As the world continuously journeys through technological evolution, VR in talent acquisition has proven to be more than just a tantalizing premise. It is indeed a steely, palpable pathway with measureless potential—heralding a new era in the talent acquisition saga.

Chapter 5. The Integration of Virtual Reality in the Recruitment Process

The potential of Virtual Reality (VR) in recruitment is immense, revolutionizing everything from job postings, interviews, to candidate assessments. By implementing VR, companies can create more engaging, authentic, and comprehensive recruiting processes.

5.1. The Concept of VR in Recruitment

Virtual Reality, at its most basic, is a simulation of a three-dimensional environment that users can interact with in a seemingly real or physical way via a special electronic device, usually a headset. It offers a 360-degree immersive experience that can teleport individuals into various scenarios or environments. These environments can range from realistic to entirely fabricated but still engross just the user. In recruitment, this technology can be leveraged for a variety of innovative applications.

5.2. Virtual Job Tryouts

Imagine being able to immerse your job candidates in the actual roles they've applied for. With VR, it's entirely possible. It can simulate the work environment, job tasks, and challenges, allowing candidates to demonstrate their skills and abilities in a realistic and immersive setting. For example, a first-year medical resident can perform a virtual surgery, or a sales executive can navigate a complex negotiation scenario. This kind of simulation gives both the employer and the candidate significant advantages. Employers can more accurately assess a candidate's skills and adaptability, while the candidate gets a clear view of their job role and its demands.

Virtual job tryouts not only make the recruitment process more engaging but also more effective. They provide a more holistic view of a candidate, going beyond traditional paper-based assessments or interviews.

5.3. VR in Interviews

VR can also be used to conduct virtual interviews. Candidates can engage with interviewers as avatars in a VR environment, entirely from the comfort of their homes. It saves travel time and expenses for both candidates and businesses, especially in initial rounds, and provides a unique experience that could differentiate an employer in a competitive job market.

Moreover, interviews conducted in VR can be gamified. Scenario-based interviewing through VR can be engaging, fun, and effective in assessing the candidate's behavior in certain situations. As with virtual job tryouts, VR interviews offer greater insights into candidates' skills and operational adaptability.

5.4. Employer Branding and Virtual Tours

In the competitive environment of recruitment, employer branding is essential to attract and retain the most talented individuals. VR can offer compelling, interactive experiences that showcase a company's culture, values, and work environment. Candidates can take VR tours of the office, meet their potential colleagues, and even experience a typical day in the life at the company. This immersive experience can offer candidates a realistic view of what it would be like to work for the organization.

Apart from attracting candidates, VR can also be beneficial in improving retention rates. A candidate who has a clear, realistic understanding of the job role and work environment is more likely to remain in the position longer.

5.5. VR in Candidate Assessment

VR allows hiring managers to test potential employees in practical, real-world situations, helping them assess a candidate's skills and competencies accurately. Through VR, companies can measure how candidates handle pressure, how they solve problems, and how they collaborate with others, all in a controlled environment.

VR assessments are not only accurate but also fair, reducing unconscious bias in the hiring process. The VR environment treats all candidates the same way, without biases for age, race, gender, and physical appearance that can sometimes inadvertently affect an interviewer's judgment.

5.6. Challenges and Opportunities

Despite its significant potential, VR in recruitment is still a relatively new concept and has its challenges. Notably, it requires substantial investment in hardware and software, calling for a careful cost-benefit analysis. Additionally, it also poses a learning curve, training both recruiters and candidates to handle the new technology.

Yet, the opportunities VR presents outweigh the challenges. As technology becomes cheaper and more accessible, companies can expect a significant return on investment from VR recruitment. VR could potentially redefine recruitment, placing companies that embrace it at the forefront of talent acquisition.

In conclusion, VR offers a brave new world in recruitment. From immersive job tryouts to interactive tours, it can deliver an authentic, engaging, and efficient recruitment process that attracts and retains the best candidates. With businesses continuously seeking an edge in recruitment, VR technology stands out as one of the most promising pathways to the future of talent acquisition.

Chapter 6. Using VR for Skill Assessment and Selection

Ever since Virtual Reality (VR) has made its breathtaking entrance into the world of technology, it has proven its incredible adaptability. Beyond providing immersive video game experiences or transforming our entertainment habits, VR is rapidly infiltrating corporate chambers, particularly reshaping the landscape of Human Resources (HR). When thinking specifically about skill assessment and selection, VR offers a whole new realm of innovation and efficiency.

6.1. The Dawn of VR in Skill Assessment

It all started in the late 2010s when HR professionals recognized the potential VR held for skill assessments. Initially used in high-risk industry sectors such as aviation and medicine for training and simulation purposes, VR quickly found its way into the HR industry.

HR requires both a scientific and human approach, as it is all about evaluating an individual's capability of handling tasks mindfully. Thus, it is only natural that VR, which simulates real-world conditions with the utmost precision, has been recognized as a viable tool for accurate and immersive evaluations.

Consider, for example, the use of VR in imparting and assessing soft skills. This typically involves creating scenarios that test an individual's communication, problem-solving, and leadership skills. Unlike traditional methods, VR can faithfully reproduce lifelike situations where candidates are evaluated based on their performance under realistic conditions, making it a valuable addition to the HR toolbox.

6.2. Harnessing the Power of VR for Skills Assessment

As VR technology evolves, it presents exciting opportunities for assessing technical and job-specific skills in real-time. This delivers a more accurate picture of a candidate's ability to navigate specific job-related challenges. For jobs that require mechanical skills, such as technicians or engineers, VR can help test the candidate's precision and efficiency in performing certain tasks.

For salespeople or customer service representatives, VR's potential lies in its ability to simulate client interactions or sales pitches. With companies like STRIVR leading the way, VR can allow candidates to demonstrate their capabilities in dealing with different customer personas accurately.

VR can also be instrumental in testing a candidate's ability to handle stressful situations. The immersive nature of VR can simulate high-pressure circumstances, providing a platform for candidates to demonstrate their stress management and decision-making abilities. For roles where crisis management is crucial, such as first responders or medical professionals, VR could be of paramount importance.

6.3. Implementing VR in the Selection Process

The integration of VR in the selection process provides a powerful and innovative means of candidate engagement. Not only does it offer an engaging candidate experience, but it also allows companies to showcase their technological prowess. However, integrating VR into your selection process is not without its challenges.

Firstly, you will need to determine the technical requirements and ensure you have access to the right hardware and software. This will include VR headsets and potentially specialized devices depending on the type of VR you choose to deploy. For example, room-scale VR may require additional devices beyond just a headset.

Secondly, creating VR experiences is typically time-consuming and costly. However, partnerships with tech companies that specialize in VR can mitigate these challenges. It is important to select a partner who understands the specific needs of your organization and can create customized experiences.

There are also ethical considerations around the use of VR. This includes ensuring that users feel safe when they are immersed in a VR experience and that their performance is evaluated fairly.

6.4. Real-world Examples: VR in Action for Recruitment and Selection

We have seen many successful implementations of VR for skill assessment and evaluation. In the automotive industry, Ford has used VR to test prospective employees' assembly line skills. Jaguar Land Rover has taken a gamification approach, creating an application called "Code Breaker" to engage and test candidates' coding and problem-solving abilities.

In the retail industry, Walmart has deployed VR effectively for employee training and assessment. Using VR headsets, potential and existing employees experience customer service scenarios and are evaluated based on their responses. This not only increases the variety of situations that can be tested but also provides a more realistic assessment of employee capabilities.

Similarly, Deutsche Bahn has used VR in recruitment events to give potential employees a 360-degree tour of their working environment and gauge their aptitude for specific roles within the company.

6.5. Strategizing VR Deployment for Skill Assessment and Selection

It's crucial to strategize for the successful adoption of VR. Firstly, identify the skills or roles suited for VR assessment - whether technical, soft, or crisis management skills. Then, consider your budget and identify the right tools or partnership for creating VR experiences.

Moreover, ensure you have the correct protocols in place to ensure fairness and transparency in the assessment process, addressing any prejudices or biases that may occur. Keep the experience user-friendly, ensuring candidates are comfortable with the technology.

Lastly, always be open to changes and improvements. The VR industry is constantly evolving. Therefore, it pays off to remain updated with the latest trends and applications to ensure your VR skill assessment and selection strategies stay relevant and effective.

6.6. VR: The Future of Recruitment and Selection

The future holds exciting possibilities for VR in recruitment and selection. As technology continues to evolve, we will see VR become more accessible, more immersive, and less expensive, which will only increase its functionality in recruitment and selection.

In conclusion, the rise of Virtual Reality is not just a passing trend. For HR professionals looking to streamline and innovate their recruitment process, VR provides an effective, engaging, and future-forward solution. By integrating VR into skill assessments and selection, companies can provide realistic, immersive experiences that accurately evaluate the skills and potential of candidates in a dynamic and engaging way - this lays the foundation for smarter recruitment, better talent management, and ultimately, a stronger workforce.

Chapter 7. Case Studies: Success Stories of VR in Hiring

In recent years, many organizations have started leveraging Virtual Reality (VR) technology in their pursuit to attract, assess, and select talent in innovative ways. Here we showcase case studies illustrating the transformative potential of VR in the recruitment realm, each of which could serve as an inspirational guide for HR professionals contemplating integrating VR into their recruitment strategy.

Let's dive into the real-world experiences of pioneering companies that have effectively employed VR in their hiring processes.

7.1. Case Study 1: Jaguar Land Rover

The British multinational automotive company, Jaguar Land Rover, introduced a recruiting challenge in 2017, in collaboration with the virtual band Gorillaz. Prospects were tasked with cracking code in a two-part mixed reality app. The first part involved assembling the Jaguar I-PACE concept car and the second part included a series of puzzles set in a 360° environment.

The company's initial goal was to recruit more than 1,000 electronic and software engineers to support its autonomous, connected cars and electrification program. However, this unique strategy proved highly effective, providing a broader insight into an applicant's capabilities than a traditional CV or interview might.

7.2. Case Study 2: Siemens Graduate Program

Siemens revolutionized its Graduate Program recruitment process by integrating VR technology. The company created a virtual factory tour that enabled candidates to explore an interactive Siemens factory environment. This VR tour offered applicants an immersive experience of what it was like to work at Siemens, from the cutting-edge technology in use to the collaborative work culture. This level of immersion offered candidates an opportunity to assess their fit within the organization, thereby improving the quality of talent attraction.

7.3. Case Study 3: Commonwealth Bank of Australia

The Commonwealth Bank of Australia (CBA) utilized VR technology to provide an innovative approach to graduate recruitment. Candidates were given a Samsung Gear VR headset to witness a day in the life at CBA. The VR experience highlighted the bank's innovative workspaces, culture, and the scope of work involved with various roles. The virtual tour received positive feedback for its immersive quality and appeal to young candidates, demonstrating the benefits of VR for candidate engagement.

7.4. Case Study 4: L'Oreal

Beauty giant L'Oreal made a dive into VR by utilizing the technology to simulate job experiences for potential interns and employees. Candidates were given a realistic, 360° look at life in the company's offices and labs. This immersive VR experience served as a stepping stone towards creating a recruitment process that was dynamic, innovative, and able to draw in a tech-savvy workforce.

7.5. Case Study 5: British Army

The British Army embarked on a campaign to increase recruitment, which included the use of VR in their selection process. The VR experience allowed potential recruits to participate in a combat training simulation, offering unique insights into what the role genuinely entailed. This not only enriched the candidate experience but also provided a more authentic understanding of job expectations.

7.6. Case Study 6: U.S. Navy

The U.S. Navy used VR technology to engage visitors at the 2017 Fleet Week New York. They offered a firsthand experience of a Navy ship in high seas, with the ship handlers facing a variety of operational scenarios. This VR exposure provided potential recruits with insights into the Navy's operations and work environment—critical information for making informed career decisions.

In conclusion, VR in recruitment allows prospective employees to experience the work environment, operations, and culture of the employing organization ahead of time, which substantially impacts their decision-making process. This concept's adoption has gradually increased, given its success in companies like Jaguar Land Rover, Siemens, Commonwealth Bank of Australia, L'Oreal, the British Army, and the U.S. Navy. These case studies serve as substantial evidence that HR can improve the effectiveness of their recruitment and selection process by integrating innovative technologies like VR.

Looking forward, VR is set to become an integral part of recruitment strategies, with its immersive experiences bringing life and appeal to standardized, often monotonous processes. Seeing how the early adopters have benefited from the technology, it's expected that more businesses will follow suit, leading to a complete transformation in how talent attraction, selection, and retention are managed.

Chapter 8. VR Transforming Employee Onboarding and Training

The metamorphosis of virtual reality from a gaming novelty to a business transformation tool has been nothing short of astounding. One crucial area that has witnessed a ripple effect of this technological advances is in employee onboarding and training. VR presents a brilliant opportunity to deliver engaging, interactive, accessible, and efficient training programs to new hires as well as existing employees, thus revolutionizing age-old onboarding and training methods.

8.1. The Paradigm Shift to Immersive Learning

For generations, organizations have struggled with traditional onboarding and training methods such as lectures, presentations, and written materials, which often led to information overload and disengagement. Research shows that humans remember 10% of what they read, 20% of what they hear, but up to 90% of what they do or simulate.

Enter Virtual Reality (VR). The technology's immersive nature makes it an excellent tool for learning and comprehension. VR places learners in the middle of the action, implementing the "learning by doing" methodology. It's like moving from reading about swimming to diving into the water.

Furthermore, unlike traditional methods, VR makes learning fun and interactive, leading to increased engagement levels. The user is no longer a passive recipient but an active participant in the training scenario.

8.2. Simplifying Complex Concepts

In numerous fields such as engineering, healthcare, and advanced manufacturing, employees often need to understand complex concepts and machinery that are challenging to explain using traditional training methods. VR can turn complex concepts into immersive demonstrations, allowing trainees to interact with life-size, 3D models, and witness processes firsthand, thereby enhancing their understanding. This experiential form of learning significantly improves retention and ability to apply knowledge.

8.3. Real-World Simulation and Skill Development

VR enables companies to create realistic simulations of their work environments. New employees can practice new tasks, master new skills, and familiarize themselves with workflow processes without the risk of costly or dangerous mistakes.

Take the case of Walmart. The retail giant has successfully implemented VR to train over one million employees across its various locations. Using VR headsets, associates undergo immersive training that simulates real-life customer situations, helping them better handle Black Friday sales rush, for instance.

Similarly, VR is used in hazardous professions such as firefighting, chemical manufacturing, and surgery, where even a slight error can be catastrophic. Implementing VR in training offers a safe and controlled environment to practice critical skills.

8.4. Equipment and Location Independence

One of the notable benefits of VR-based training is its independence from specific locations and equipment. VR can simulate any environment, from manufacturing plants to office spaces, irrespective of the trainee's location. This flexibility is particularly helpful for multinationals with globally dispersed workforce or for remote workers, eliminating expensive and time-consuming travel.

8.5. Customized Learning Experience

VR's adaptability allows for a tailored learning experience. Companies can adjust the complexity level to match each learner's proficiency, enable learners to repeat scenarios until they master them, and provide instant feedback which aids in learning reinforcement. This ability to personalize training makes VR an invaluable tool in modern HR practices.

8.6. Bridging the Confidence Gap

New employees often struggle with a confidence gap when starting a new job, due to unfamiliarity with the workspace or the job role. VR onboarding can help bridge this gap as it gives new hires a chance to explore their work environment virtually, meet their virtual colleagues, and even practice their daily tasks before the first day at work, thereby boosting their confidence.

8.7. Challenges of Implementing VR

Despite the myriad benefits, the incorporation of VR into onboarding and training isn't without its challenges. These include high upfront costs, need for technical expertise, possibility of cyber-sickness, and resistance from employees who are less tech-savvy. However, as VR technology continues to advance and become more mainstream, these barriers are likely to lessen.

8.8. Future of VR in Employee Onboarding and Training

Companies that have adopted VR in onboarding and training are reaping considerable benefits, as studies show a notable improvement in knowledge retention, skill application, and overall learning experience. As technology becomes more accessible and affordable, we can only expect its adoption rate to rise.

Moreover, ongoing advancements indicate the possibility of multi-user VR scenarios, where multiple employees from different locations could participate in the same simulation, fostering teamwork and collaboration. This advancement could bring a revolution in terms of remote training and team building, making the future of VR in employee onboarding and training even more promising.

In conclusion, VR's transformational potential in employee onboarding and training is undeniable. However, as with all new technology implementations, an organization should consider its unique needs, workforce familiarity with technology, budget, and desired outcomes before choosing to jump on the VR bandwagon in HR. It's evident that VR isn't just a fad — it's an investment in the future of effective and engaging employee onboarding and training.

Chapter 9. Double-Edged Sword: The Pros and Cons of VR in HR

Virtual reality, often referred to by its acronym VR, is a burgeoning technology making significant strides in the corporate world. It is particularly becoming popular in the realm of Human Resources (HR), where it is transforming traditional practices such as recruitment and selection. Yet, like any technological innovation, VR brings with it both immense potentialities and substantial challenges.

9.1. Understanding Virtual Reality

Before evaluating the pros and cons of VR in HR, it's crucial to understand precisely what this technology entails. VR refers to a simulated experience created by utilizing computer software and hardware. It can replicate an environment exactly or create an entirely new world, all while allowing the user to interact with that environment in a seemingly real and physical way. Shortly, this technology will not only provide visual and auditory input but also cater to other senses, such as touch, to create an all-encompassing virtual experience.

9.2. The Pros of VR in HR

As much as virtual reality is a product of the digital era, it is also a key driver pushing the boundaries of this very era. Let's explore some benefits of integrating VR in HR practices, particularly in recruitment and selection.

9.2.1. Enhanced Applicant Experience

One of the groundbreaking advantages of VR in HR lies in its ability to enrich the applicant experience. Instead of generic company descriptions and lengthy procedure explanations, candidates can be virtually immersed in the company culture and the actual job environment. This realistic job preview helps potential employees to get a clearer and more truthful image of what working at a company entails, leading to more effective self-selection processes.

9.2.2. Efficient Skill Assessment

VR technology enables recruiters to assess candidates' skills in a more realistic and immersive setting. Through VR, potential employees can be put in simulated job situations where they would need to react in real-time, allowing recruiters to assess their responses. This practical assessment is far superior to traditional interview questions and can predict on-the-job performance more accurately.

9.2.3. Lower Recruitment Costs

Traditionally, recruitment involves travel costs, particularly when the potential talent pool is geographically diverse. However, with VR-enabled interviews, companies can save on the cost of face-to-face interviews, which include applicant travel expenses, room rentals and often, lost work hours.

9.3. The Cons of VR in HR

Despite its numerous advantages, integrating VR into HR is not without its challenges and drawbacks. Below are some of the most significant considerations to take into account.

9.3.1. High Initial Costs

While VR can result in cost savings in the long run, the initial investment required to set up VR infrastructure can be substantial. This includes the cost of purchasing VR headsets and developing custom-made VR programs, costs which may not be feasible for all organizations, particularly start-ups and SMEs.

9.3.2. Technical Glitches and Uncertainty

Like any developing technology, VR systems are not immune to technical glitches. Similarly, the VR technological landscape changes rapidly, and therefore there is a degree of uncertainty concerning obsolescence and the need for constant upgrading.

9.3.3. Lack of Personal Interaction

Despite all the realism it can provide, VR still lacks the warmth of human connection. Body language, micro-expressions, and the overall 'vibe' are integral to the interviewer-interviewee rapport. While VR does offer a unique, immersive experience, these in-person subtleties may still elude it.

To conclude, VR presents a double-edged sword for HR professions. Its innovative potential to revolutionize recruitment and selection is undeniable. Nonetheless, a careful cost-benefit analysis and thoughtful strategy are required to navigate the trade-offs successfully. Ultimately, the comprehensive integration of virtual reality in HR depends on how well an organization can balance the challenges with the distinct benefits that VR brings to the table. It's a brave new world, and it calls for brave new approaches to talent acquisition.

Chapter 10. Future Perspectives: The Next Big Steps for Virtual Reality in HR

Virtual reality (VR) is on the cusp of establishing a significant foothold in the human resources (HR) industry, promising a new phase of innovation and evolution in recruitment and selection. The implications are far-reaching and transformative. Tasks that were previously seen as resource-intensive or wide open to human bias and error can now be handled with greater objectivity and efficiency. By stepping into the future with VR technology, HR can access a wealth of benefits capable of shifting its operations to a higher gear.

10.1. Advancing Efficiency in Recruitment

Embracing VR means turning a rather opaque process of recruitment into a transparent and error-minimizing activity. Consider the traditional interview scenario. Interviews are typically subjective, with potential biases influencing decisions that can lead to costly mis-hires.

VR gives the potential for creating an objective, standardized environment where candidates around the globe can be observed and their responses analyzed in a like-for-like manner. In addition to reducing bias, VR can bring efficiency in terms of saved time and cost. Virtual interviews reduce the need for space and travel, in turn cutting down on logistical costs and strengthening the bottom line.

According to experts, VR can even help organizations identify top talent quickly. In a McKinsey & Company report, it was suggested that VR could enable employers to analyze applicants' emotional reactions to scenarios and their approach to problem-solving. By analyzing facial expressions, body language, and interactions with the environment, recruiters can make a more nuanced evaluation of potential employees, contributing to a more qualified and skilled workforce.

10.2. Revolutionizing Job Trials

Job trials have always been a weak point in the recruitment process. They are inherently problematic, given that they attempt to replicate an entire job role in a short span, consequently failing to capture an accurate assessment of a job applicant's capabilities in the actual role.

VR has proven itself to be a game-changer here. It allows organizations to create realistic, immersive job simulations where candidates can virtually experience a day in the life of the role they are applying for. From simulating high-pressure scenarios in airline pilot recruitment to mimicking customer service environments, VR can provide a detailed understanding of the applicant's strengths and weaknesses.

VR tool STRIVR is one such instance, which can create custom job trials and environments for various industries and has demonstrated the ability to accurately predict candidates' job performance. This revolutionizes the very concept of a job trial, increasing its reliability as a selection technique.

10.3. Enhancing Candidate Experience

First impressions matter significantly in the recruitment process.

Candidates' perception of an organization can be deeply affected by their experience during the recruitment process. Here, VR demonstrates another value proposition.

VR can create a distinct, immersive, and interactive 'pre-boarding' experience for a candidate. Job seekers can 'walk through' the virtual office, meet with potential colleagues, explore the work environment, and even participate in virtual team activities. These experiences give candidates a sense of what it's like to work there, contributing to a positive image of the employer brand. Moreover, the novelty factor of VR can leave a lasting memorable experience, setting the company apart in a competitive job market.

10.4. Enhancing Diversity and Inclusion

Efforts to build a diverse and inclusive workforce can significantly benefit from the use of VR in recruitment. As already mentioned, VR can minimize human bias that may inadvertently creep into traditional recruitment processes, resulting in a more diverse hiring pool.

Furthermore, VR can simulate scenarios to help evaluators understand how candidates handle situations related to diversity and inclusion, providing an insight into their behaviors and attitudes. This would be otherwise difficult to evaluate in a traditional interview setup.

10.5. The Road Ahead: Challenges and Opportunities

While the advantages of integrating VR into HR are numerous, it's also important to be cognizant of the challenges it poses. The most prominent is the digital divide. Not all candidates have access to VR technology or are adept in using it. Consequently, relying too heavily on VR for recruitment might exclude these segments of job seekers.

Secondly, VR scenarios, while impressively realistic, are still simulations. They might not completely encapsulate the nuances of real-life scenarios or the multifaceted nature of jobs. Training evaluators to accurately evaluate performance in VR can also be a challenge.

However, these hurdles shouldn't dissuade HR from exploring VR's potential. Its capacity to revolutionize recruitment is immense, and with increasing technology accessibility and VR software becoming more advanced and nuanced, many of these challenges can be resolved over time.

Innovation is inevitable, and VR is leading this charge in the HR space. Companies that embrace this technology now will have the advantage of not only engaging with top talent in creative ways today but also developing and refining best practices for the future. Today's pioneering steps in VR for recruitment and selection might well be tomorrow's industry gold standard.

Let's not forget that the future of HR lies in talent's hands. Those who are joining the workforce now are tech natives—they grew up with social media, smartphones, and are comfortable with emerging technologies like VR. By integrating VR into HR operations, organizations can 'speak the same language' as these new workforces, making them feel understood and valued.

As we navigate through the Fourth Industrial Revolution, it's clear that the intersection of technology and HR is at the heart of this rapid transformation. VR marks the next big step in this progress, and HR has the opportunity to step boldly towards it. VR is not just the wave of the future—it's here now, and HR must learn how to navigate its possibilities today to make waves of their own tomorrow.

In conclusion, the future of VR in HR practice is undoubtedly rich and exciting, one that promises to enhance the quality of talent, streamline processes, and augment the very essence of HR practice. HR practitioners must thus be ready to ride this advancing tide that seeks to transform HR from within. Engage with the possibilities, explore this new frontier, and make VR a part of your strategic HR blueprint to stay ahead in the talent game.

Chapter 11. Strategic Guidelines for Implementing VR in Your HR Department

An understanding of the guidelines for implementing Virtual Reality (VR) in your HR Department is crucial to maximize the benefits of this innovative and immersive technology. These guidelines are provided in an effort to create a holistic view, accounting for tactical, strategic, and practical considerations.

11.1. Identifying the Need for VR

Understanding the need for integrating VR technology into the HR department is the initial step. Be clear on your needs - whether it be for recruitment, training, talent retention, or improving team collaborations. VR technology can be applied to numerous functions across HR, clarifying its role for your HR programs is essential.

11.2. Understanding the Basics of VR Technology

Before embracing VR technology, a thorough understanding is important. Get familiar with common terms like augmented reality (AR), VR, mixed reality (MR). Fully understand the benefits and limitations of each technology to shape its application in your HR department.

11.3. Choosing the Right VR Technology

There exist several VR solutions tailored for different purposes. Your choice depends on what your HR department seeks to achieve. Given the myriad of options, be clear on the features that you would need most.

1. Stand-alone VR devices

2. PC-based VR devices

3. Smartphone-based VR devices

Evaluate how these can contribute to your processes and decide which would be most compatible with your department's operations.

11.4. Testing VR Platforms

Always start with a pilot program to evaluate the effectiveness of your selected VR platform. It helps in spotting the challenges and addressing them before the complete implementation.

11.5. Creating Immersive Content

There's no VR experience without relevant and impactful content. You may develop your own content or collaborate with VR content providers. Keep in mind, the content should recreate realistic work situations that enable valid and meaningful assessments or experiences.

11.6. Training the Team

After establishing the system and content, it's time to train your team. Make sure everyone involved understands how to wear the headset, operate the VR system, and navigate the virtual environment.

11.7. Measuring ROI

After implementation, evaluate the success of the VR program. Assess benefits gained in terms of time saved, improved employee experiences, reduction in recruitment costs, or any other key metrics pertinent to your organization.

11.8. Adjusting Your VR Strategy

On receiving feedback, make adjustments to improve the effectiveness of your VR initiatives. This iterative process will find the version that aligns best with your HR practices, culture, and goals.

11.9. Ensuring Legal and Ethical Considerations

Lastly, it's important to address any legal and ethical considerations that come with VR. It's a new technology and laws may not be fully developed. Be transparent, respect privacy, use data responsibly, and avoid any form of discrimination.

Remember, the implementation process may have its own set of challenges. Always be ready to adapt and alter your strategy to meet your organization's specific needs. First and foremost, this should be a strategic decision that supports your HR goals.

Through careful planning, thoughtful execution, and rigorous assessment, VR can breathe new life into your HR department, changing the way we think about talent acquisition and development. With these guidelines in hand, you're well on your way to integrating VR into your HR process, all while maintaining a focus on what matters most—finding, attracting, and developing the best talent.

Stay on the front lines of HR innovation. Embrace VR and take a giant stride into the future of talent management!